THE TOP TEN GROSSEST ANIMALS

whitestar kids

LET'S START!

IT MAY SEEM STRANGE, BUT SOME ANIMALS SEEM COMPLETELY AT HOME AMONGST POOP AND VOMIT, OTHERS HAVE NO PROBLEM USING THEIR OWN TONGUE TO CLEAN THEIR EARS, AND OTHERS SHOOT SNOT BOMBS FROM THEIR NOSES!

But you need to remember that, though many of these behaviors may seem revolting to us, they are actually necessary for the animal's survival. Which one is actually the most "disgusting"? There are plenty vying for the title!

COME ON, BE BRAVE AND READ OUR RATINGS.

DISGUSTING FEATURE

FUN FACT

Look for these symbols to discover some unexpected **FUN FACTS** and which **DISGUSTING FEATURES** have won these **TEN ANIMALS** such unenviable rankings!

THE LEVEL OF DISGUST WILL GROW FROM POSITION 10 TO THE TERRIBLE 1!

At the bottom of the page, you will find the names of the **TEN ANIMALS**. Try and guess their rankings and write down which name you think matches each position. **AS YOU READ THE BOOK, YOU WILL FIND OUT HOW MANY YOU GOT RIGHT!**

1 ________________

2 ________________

3 ________________

4 ________________

5 ________________

6 ________________

7 ________________

8 ________________

9 ________________

10 ________________

- **FULMAR**
- **SKUNK**
- **TURKEY VULTURE**
- **GIRAFFE**
- **MARINE IGUANA**
- **TEXAS HORNED LIZARD**
- **BLACK WIDOW**
- **KOALA**
- **LLAMA**
- **STARFISH**

NUMBER

10 GIRAFFE

SCIENTIFIC NAME:
Giraffa camelopardalis

SIZE: 18.7 ft (5.7 m)

It's not just the neck and legs. Giraffes also have a very long **TONGUE.**
It can reach up to a foot and a half (45 cm) in length and is the perfect instrument for ripping away the spiny leaves from the acacia tree.
Giraffes also love doing something else with their tongue: they stick it in their **NOSE** to lick away the **SNOT**.
And while they are cleaning their nose, they also take advantage to clean their **EARS**, just to get rid of some of the **WAX**.

DIET:
plants, cannot resist acacia leaves

HABITAT:
Africa,
in the savanna

DISGUSTING FEATURE

They clean their nose and ears with their tongue.

FUN FACT

Giraffes are the tallest animal in the world.

NUMBER

9 SKUNK

SCIENTIFIC NAME:
Mephitis mephitis

SIZE: 30 in (80 cm)

This elegant-looking animal has a **NOXIOUS** secret weapon. It has a gland near its anus that produces an **OILY YELLOW LIQUID** with a nauseating odor and a long-lasting irritating effect, which the animal **SPRAYS** at whatever annoys or scares it. If you see a skunk lifting its tail, it is time to move away, slowly and quietly. Whatever ends up in its line of fire will have a lot to do to get rid of the **STINK**.

DIET:
small animals, fruits, and roots

HABITAT:
North and South America, in forests and plains

DISGUSTING FEATURE
Sprays a stinky liquid from its bottom.

FUN FACT
The jet can be launched from more than 10 feet (3 m) away.

NUMBER

8 LLAMA

SCIENTIFIC NAME:
Lama glama

If they don't like someone, llamas **SPIT** at them. As they do to those members who are beneath them, so that it is clear who has the **AUTHORITY** within the group. And females are no better: when they refuse a courtship, they spit at males to spurn them.
Spitting is also a good way to show **IRRITATION**, and when they get really angry, llamas start spitting a **STINKY GREEN LIQUID** that they regurgitate from their stomach.

DIET:
hay, grass, and leaves that they chew and chew and chew...

HABITAT:
South America, in the mountain plains

DISGUSTING FEATURE

Spits and vomits on others.

FUN FACT

They are resilient and move in rocky, high-altitude places with ease.

LOTS OF DROOL AND SALIVA

Saliva is certainly one of the most **DISGUSTING** bodily fluids. It is very useful while eating as it makes it easier for us to swallow food, yet we think of it as slimy and **STICKY** and we don't really like to touch it.

IN THE ANIMAL KINGDOM, HOWEVER, DROOL AND SALIVA ARE USED MORE OFTEN THAN YOU MIGHT THINK. HERE ARE SOME EXAMPLES:

Slime trails

Everyone knows about **SLUGS** and **SNAILS**. They produce slime in abundance and immerse their entire body in it. In this way, they use the **VISCOUS** element of the liquid to slide more easily on the ground.

Sometimes, the animals produce so much slime that they actually leave a trail of it behind them.

The slime protects snails from harmful bacteria and sunlight.

You do what you can!

KANGAROOS are athletic animals, but, living in a dry environment, they really suffer from the heat. To find relief, they soak themselves in their own saliva, in particular by **LICKING** their arms. As it evaporates, the aqueous component of the saliva slightly lowers the kangaroo's body **TEMPERATURE**, giving it a little cool relief.

They regurgitate the vegetation they eat, chew it some more, and then swallow it for final digestion.

They use their tail like a fifth leg.

With a name like that...

The **SPITTLEBUG** is a small insect that, while in its **LARVA** state, builds a shelter on a plant, producing a **SOFT** and **FOAMY** substance very similar to a spit of saliva.
Which is where it got its name!

The foam is formed by passing liquid excrement and air through the abdomen.

The nest of slime is also ideal for maintaining the perfect temperature.

NUMBER

7 MARINE IGUANA

SCIENTIFIC NAME: *Amblyrhynchus cristatus*

SIZE: 4 ft (1.2 m)

The rather hideous appearance of these animals is nothing compared to their disgusting habit of launching **WHITE SPURTS OF STICKY MUCUS** from their nose. Unfortunately, it is the only way they can eliminate the **SALT** absorbed while diving in the sea.

In fact, above their eyes are **SALINE GLANDS** connected to the nostrils. When these organs are full, the iguanas expel the excess salt by powerfully **SNEEZING**.

DIET:
algae they graze underwater

HABITAT:
South America, Galápagos Islands, on rocky coasts

DISGUSTING FEATURE

Continuously sneezes very salty white mucus.

FUN FACT

It can last underwater for up to 30 minutes grazing on algae.

NUMBER

6 FULMAR

SCIENTIFIC NAME:
Fulmarus glacialis

SIZE: 20 in (50 cm)

What makes this elegant bird so repugnant? It's simple: it defends itself with **VOMIT**. In fact, it knows how to keep predators at bay by shooting projectiles of particularly nauseating, **OILY VOMIT**. Even the chicks use this defense strategy: from as young as two weeks old they are left alone in the nest while their parents go in search of food. This **STOMACH FLUID** then sticks to the unfortunate victim, who finds it extremely difficult to remove the horrible substance.

DIET:
fish

HABITAT:
along the marine coasts of the North Atlantic Ocean

DISGUSTING FEATURE

To defend itself, it launches an oily vomit at its predators.

FUN FACT

Its name derives from an ancient Icelandic word meaning "repugnant seagull."

NUMBER

5 TEXAS HORNED LIZARD

SCIENTIFIC NAME:
Phrynosoma cornutum

SIZE: 4.5 in (11 cm)

Woe to those who make him angry! Not only are the **EYES** of this little reptile bloodshot, but they actually **SPLASH** blood in all directions. It is sprayed with surprising **POWER**, reaching up to more than 5 feet (1.5 m), often ending up in the eyes of the predator, who is left **BLINDED** for a few moments. The blood is not toxic, but the **SHOCK** effect gives the lizard time to run away.

DIET:
insects and other small arthropods

HABITAT:
North America, in arid environments

DISGUSTING FEATURE

Blood spurts from its eyes.

FUN FACT

It can inflate its body by drawing air into its lungs.

ONLY FOR THE STRONGEST STOMACHS

Is the idea of something feeding on blood rather strange to you? If you think about it, blood is a high-energy drink, but it is also very difficult to get hold of.

ANYTHING THAT FEEDS ON BLOOD HAS TO DO IT QUIETLY, WITHOUT THE VICTIM EVEN NOTICING. THEY ALSO NEED A POINTED OR SHARP MOUTH AND SUBSTANCES TO KEEP THE BLOOD FLUID AS THEY DRINK IT.

Vampire bat

Little **VAMPIRE BATS** live in South America and really go crazy for the blood of cattle and some birds. They land on the body of a **SLEEPING** animal, find a vein under the skin, and then bite down with their **SHARP LITTLE TEETH**, drinking a small amount of blood from the wound.

The saliva of vampire bats contains DRACULIN, a substance that stops the victim's blood from coagulating.

If a vampire bat goes for two nights in a row without eating, it will starve to death.

Oxpecker

Large herbivores in the savanna are often seen giving a ride to **OXPECKERS**. These little birds remove **PARASITES** from their host's skin and any fly **LARVAE** from infected wounds.

They actually are also quite fond of blood and sometimes use their beak to keep a wound open in order to keep up a supply.

They tug out the fur of large herbivores to line their nests.

Leech

The most famous blood sucker is the **LEECH**. It sucks its host's blood by attaching to the skin with a **SUCTION CUP** and then eats enough to **INFLATE** like a balloon. This animal has been used in the past by doctors to remove the excess blood accumulating in patients' wounds.

It can suck enough blood to grow to 10 times its start weight.

It has 10 eyes, 6 hearts, 32 brains, and 10 sacs to store the blood.

NUMBER

4 TURKEY VULTURE

SCIENTIFIC NAME:
Cathartes aura

SIZE:
30 in (80 cm)

For this bird, **POOPING ON ITSELF** isn't an embarrassing accident, but a very useful solution! Thanks to the huge amount of **ACID** contained within its feces, by dirtying its feet with its own excrement the vulture in fact **DISINFECTS** them.
This is important because as it scavenges the carcasses of dead animals in search of food, the bird's body picks up a huge amount of **BACTERIA**, which can only be eliminated in this way.

DIET:
mainly dead animals

HABITAT:
North and
South America,
in all environments

DISGUSTING FEATURE

It poops on its own feet, and when it feels threatened, it vomits on whoever is annoying it.

FUN FACT

It flies at low altitudes in order to smell the gasses produced during decomposition.

DO YOU NEED TO PEE?

PEE is a waste material that we eliminate quickly in the form of a liquid of a rather... **PUNGENT ODOR**.

Nice to meet you, dolphin!

Underwater life has meant that dolphins have lost the ability to **SMELL**. So, in order to recognize each other – even without seeing or hearing – they **TASTE THE URINE** of new arrivals.

By tasting pee, dolphins can understand if the animal they are faced with is a friend or foe.

They communicate their own identity through a specific sound, much like we do when we say our own name.

Each in his own way!

You may be surprised to learn that some animals don't produce **PEE** as we would normally imagine. For example, the **CHINESE SOFTSHELL TURTLE** spurts its urine from its **MOUTH**. When caught short on land, this turtle looks for the nearest puddle, sticks its head in, and... goes.

Nevertheless, as soon as it is done peeing, it never forgets to wash out its mouth!

Its shell is soft but very resistant.

Rather "unkingly" behavior

Lions wander the savanna **SPRAYING URINE** on trees, bushes, and rocks. The idea is to leave a very clear message to its peers who will smell the **STINK**: strangers are forbidden to enter this area as it **BELONGS** to whoever peed here.

The habit of covering everything with the smell of one's pee is rather usual amongst animals.

The jet of urine can reach more than 10 feet (3 m) in distance.

NUMBER

3 STARFISH

SCIENTIFIC NAME:
Asteroidea (class)

SIZE: 8 in (20 cm)

Having a **MOUTH TOO SMALL** for large prey is not a problem for many species of starfish. In fact, this echinoderm simply releases its entire **STOMACH** from its body, using it to envelop the animal it is about to eat.

At this point, the organ releases **DIGESTIVE ACIDS** that begin to **DISSOLVE** the victim. Once the victim has been reduced to a soft, shapeless mass, the starfish retracts its stomach to complete **DIGESTION**.

DIET:
echinoderms (urchins, sea cucumbers) and mollusks

HABITAT:
rocky beds of seas and oceans around the world

DISGUSTING FEATURE

Ejects its stomach to digest its prey.

FUN FACT

In summer it reproduces by dividing its body in two and then regrowing the missing arms on each part.

STOMACH AND GASTRIC JUICES

The stomach produces gastric juices, which envelop the ingested food and allow digestion and the absorption of nutrients.

ANIMALS OFTEN USE VOMITING AND STOMACH REFLUX FOR THE MOST VARIED RANGE OF REASONS.

Homemade baby food

PIGEON MILK is a liquid that is not produced in the animal's stomach but inside its **CROP**. It is formed when cells detach from the wall. These are full of fats and proteins and form a high-energy liquid, a sort of **HOMOGENIZED** product produced by the parents to nourish the little ones as soon as they hatch from the egg.

Pigeon milk is regurgitated by the parent into the baby's mouth.

"Crop milk" is also produced by flamingos and emperor penguins.

Vomit soup!

The housefly has no teeth, so it vomits its **GASTRIC JUICE** directly onto the food it wants to eat. Then, as soon as the meal has reached a soft consistency, it sucks it with its **PROBOSCIS**. The food it swallows, therefore, is already digested and is expelled in the form of **FECES** in a very short time, often while the fly is still eating.

They taste food with their feet, stepping on it several times.

The average fly will not live longer than a month.

A single mouthful

NOCTURNAL BIRDS OF PREY, like the eagle owl, swallow their prey whole and must therefore get rid of the indigestible parts, such as bones, hair, and feathers. They ball up these pieces in their stomach, ready to be vomited. In this way, they accumulate balls of dry vomit under their nests, which scientists call **WADS**.

Birds of prey produce wads every 12 hours.

The wads are studied by zoologists to find out which small animals live in the area.

NUMBER

2 BLACK WIDOW

SCIENTIFIC NAME:
Latrodectus mactans

SIZE: 0.5 in (13 mm)

To start, the black widow's hunting method is terrifying and quite **DISGUSTING**: after completely enveloping its prey in the tough threads of its **SPIDER WEB**, it then strikes it with its **SHARP FANGS**. Once its prey has been rendered totally helpless, it injects its **POISON** and waits for the chemical substances to dissolve the victim's internal organs. Only then does it tuck into its meal, **SUCKING** the prey as if it were a **MILKSHAKE**.

DIET:
other arthropods, females often eat males

HABITAT:
North America, in arid environments

DISGUSTING FEATURE
Melts its prey to suck it up.

FUN FACT
Its name comes from the females' habit of occasionally devouring the males.

NUMBER

1 KOALA

SCIENTIFIC NAME:
Phascolarctos cinereus

You weren't expecting that, were you?

SIZE: 33 in (85 cm)

Don't let yourself be fooled by appearances. One of the cutest animals in the world does something truly **DISGUSTING**: for months, a mother koala **FEEDS HER CUBS HER OWN POOP.** Although this may seem nauseating to say the least, it is actually a very useful idea. As adults, their only sustenance will be eucalyptus leaves, which are highly **TOXIC**. By eating their mommy's poop, their intestines fill with the **BACTERIA** they will need to be able to digest it.

DIET:
eucalyptus leaves, lots of eucalyptus leaves

HABITAT:
Australia, in eucalyptus forests

DISGUSTING FEATURE
Cubs eat their mommy's poop.

FUN FACT
Koalas are marsupials.

POOPS...

Even though it is our body's way of getting rid of waste, poop is still a precious resource in many ways.

THERE ARE SEVERAL ANIMALS THAT HAVE UNDERSTOOD ITS UNEXPECTED POTENTIAL! HERE ARE THREE EXAMPLES.

All animals poop, most in under 20 seconds, and many in as little as 5.

Long live poop!

The **HIPPO** is proud of its poop and is quick to show it off: it scatters it everywhere, rapidly swinging its tail as it produces it. Hippos even compete with other hippos, trying to shoot this **COMPOST SHOWER** as far as possible. This is how they **MARK THEIR TERRITORY** and show their authority.

Youngsters show respect to adults by throwing poop in their faces.

They scatter their poop to mark their territory and show their authority.

"But I thought I had already eaten that?"

RABBITS know that their poop still contains **NUTRIENTS** and so they **EAT** it again. The classic small dry, dark **BALLS** we are used to seeing lying around the ground are only formed after the **SECOND DIGESTION**.

A rabbit's teeth never stop growing and wear down as the rabbit chews.

At night, rabbits deposit a soft, sticky excrement, which they immediately eat again.

Rubic poops

Poop can also be deposited in **CUBE** form. This is how the **WOMBAT**, that graceful Australian marsupial, does it. This is because of its very slow digestion and the shape of the last section of its **INTESTINE**, which compacts the excrement into small pieces. And can you guess what wombats do with it?

Wombats stack them like BRICKS at the entrance to their den, making the opening smaller.

Wombats produce 80 to 100 cubes of poop every night.

...AND TOOTS!

Home sweet home

It's a nest made of poop, but the **OVENBIRD** is proud of it! To build it, she mixes earth, straw, and **EXCREMENT**, shaping it all into a dome. She then leaves everything to dry in the sun before laying her eggs inside. By the time the babies are born, the **STENCH** will have disappeared.

With a name like that...

These nests are the perfect temperature for eggs to grow, thanks to the fermentation of the manure.

For the **DUNG BEETLE**, poop is very important! In fact, not only does it love to eat **DUNG**, but it also feeds its young on it, and even builds them a **NEST** out of this material. This is how: the parent gathers a little poop with its feet to form a **BALL,** into which it lays an egg. When the **LARVA** is born, it will have something to eat!

Stinky grazers

Numerous **BACTERIA** live in the digestive system of **GRAZERS** such as **BISON**. Their **FERMENTATION** produces a large quantity of **INTESTINAL GASSES**, which come out as **BURPS** and **POOTS**, the smell of which is absolutely disgusting due to the **METHANE** contained. Incredible but true: these waste gasses contribute to the **GLOBAL WARMING** phenomenon of our planet.

One grazer releases between 42 and 84 gallons (160 and 320 liters) of gas into the air per day.

Mysterious signals

Living in a group means having to stay in contact with each other. **HERRING**, which swim in **SCHOOLS** made up of thousands of individuals, have found a way to do so even at night, without being able to see each other in the darkness. They emit a **FLOW OF BUBBLES AND SOUNDS** from their anus. In this way, they are able to communicate with each other without other fish understanding these **MYSTERIOUS SIGNALS**.

During the day, herring swim in deep water, while at night they rise closer to the surface.

DISGUSTING QUESTIONS

TRY TO ANSWER THESE QUESTIONS. DON'T WORRY ABOUT GETTING ANYTHING WRONG – YOU CAN FIND THE CORRECT ANSWERS ON THE NEXT PAGE!

1- WHAT PART OF THE BODY DO MALE GIRAFFES USE TO FIGHT EACH OTHER?

A Neck

B Tail

C Legs

2- WHAT ARE SKUNKS VERY SKILLED AT?

A Climbing

B Swimming

C Digging

3- WHICH LLAMA PRODUCT HAS BEEN USED FOR MORE THAN 6,000 YEARS?

A Milk

B Skin

C Wool

4- WHAT FEATURES DOES THE TAIL OF A MARINE IGUANA HAVE?

A It is flat

B It is very flexible

C It is armored

5- WHAT DO FULMARS ENRICH THEIR FISH AND MOLLUSKS DIET WITH?

A Algae

B Dead cetaceans

C Insects

6- WHAT OTHER MEANS OF DEFENSE DOES THE TEXAS HORNED LIZARD HAVE?

A Speed

B Bitter taste

C Spikes

7- WHAT ARE A TURKEY VULTURE'S MOST DEVELOPED SENSES?

A Sight and smell

B Smell and hearing

C Hearing and sight

8- AS WELL AS FOR MOVING, WHAT DOES THE STARFISH USE ITS ARMS FOR?

A To open the shells of prey

B To dig a burrow

C To protect its young

9- WHERE DO BLACK WIDOWS LAY THEIR EGGS?

A Under a leaf

B In a crack

C In a sac

10- WHAT SPECIAL FEATURES DO KOALAS HAVE?

A They bathe often

B They sleep a lot

C They never yawn

DISGUSTING ANSWERS

1-A

Male giraffes compete in tests of strength by hitting each other with their long necks. The fight ends when one of the two males gives up and leaves.

2-C

Skunks have strong feet and long nails, making them excellent diggers. They dig holes in search of grubs and earthworms.

3-C

In the Peruvian Andes, llama wool has been sheared and used to make fabrics for 6,000 years. It is light, warm, and water-repellent.

4-A

A marine iguana's tail is vertically flat to aid swimming.

5-B Fulmars are attracted by and feed on dead, stranded, or floating whales, thereby also carrying out the important role of scavengers.

6-C The body of the Texas horned lizard is covered with hard spines, making it an indigestible meal.

7-A Turkey vultures can spot a carcass while in flight at high altitudes or on the ground by following the smell of rotting meat.

8-A Starfish use their powerful arms to force the shells of mollusks such as clams and mussels open, so they can then stick their stomachs in and begin digestion.

9-C Black widows prepare a small sac smaller than half an inch (1 cm) in diameter, which can contain 200 to 250 eggs.

10-B Koalas don't have much energy and spend a lot of the time sleeping. They can snooze on branches for up to 18 hours a day.

CRISTINA BANFI

After graduating in natural sciences at the University of Milan, Cristina Banfi taught in various schools. For more than 20 years, she has worked in scientific communication and educational play and has enjoyed several editorial experiences in both scholastic and educational fields, particularly those dedicated to a young audience. In recent years, she has created several titles for White Star.

PHOTO CREDITS

Egor Arkhipov/Shutterstock: 24; Agnieszka Bacal/Shutterstock: 7; Jez Bennett/Shutterstock: 23 bottom; Uwe Bergwitz/Shutterstock: 34 top; Bradley Blackburn/Shutterstock: 3 center, 11 top; buteo/Shutterstock: 8; Jonathan Chancasana/Shutterstock: 20, 37 bottom; Yevhenii Chulovskyi/Shutterstock: 10 bottom; Aleksandar Dickov/Shutterstock: 10 top, 40; DRubi/Shutterstock: back cover bottom left, 33 top; Peter Fodor/Shutterstock: 34 bottom; Dennis Forster/Shutterstock: 35 bottom; Ian Fox/Shutterstock: 14; Hamishkun/Shutterstock: 33 bottom; Inna Horosheva/Shutterstock: 19 bottom; Irin-k/Shutterstock: 2 center, 27 top; Eric Isselee/Shutterstock: cover right center, cover left, 1 bottom, 6 left, 30, 32, 36 center; Andrea Izzotti/Shutterstock: 22; Rita_Kochmarjova/Shutterstock: cover right bottom, 1 top, 9, 36 bottom right; Mark_Kostich/Shutterstock: 29; Chloe Langton/Shutterstock: 11 bottom; Tim Malek/Shutterstock: 35 top; Maridav/Shutterstock: 13; Benny Marty/Shutterstock: 25; megscapturedtreasures/Shutterstock: 5; New Africa/Shutterstock: 27 bottom; Nancy Pauwels/Shutterstock: cover right top, 4, 36 top; Protasov AN/Shutterstock: 28; RWK007/Shutterstock: 23 top; Michael Schroeder/Shutterstock: 15; SKYDANCER/Shutterstock: 37 center bottom; slowmotiongli/Shutterstock: 31; Sompao/Shutterstock: 26 bottom; Villiers Steyn/Shutterstock: 19 top; stockphoto mania/Shutterstock: back cover bottom right, 26 top, 36 bottom left; SuperCaliPhotoListic/Shutterstock: 21; texcroc/Getty Images: 16, 37 center top; Sergey Uryadnikov/Shutterstock: 12; Nynke van Holten/Shutterstock: 3 top, 6 right; Andrei Zveaghintev/Shutterstock: back cover top, 3 bottom, 37 top; Rudmer Zwerver/Shutterstock: 18; Milan Zygmunt/Shutterstock: 17.

Editorial Coordination
Giada Francia

Design and Layout
Valentina Figus

WS whitestar kids™ is a trademark of White Star s.r.l.

Piazzale Luigi Cadorna, 6 - 20123 Milan, Italy
www.whitestar.it

Translation: Qontent
Editing: Abby Young

First printing, May 2024

ISBN 978-88-544-2100-4
1 2 3 4 5 6 28 27 26 25 24

Printed and manufactured in China by XY Cultural and Creative Park, Guangzhou

MIX
Paper from responsible sources
FSC www.fsc.org FSC® C178000